This journal belongs to:

_____

Five Minutes in the Evening

A JOURNAL FOR REST AND REFLECTION

An Hachette UK Company
www.hachette.co.uk

First published in Great Britain in 2019 by Aster, a division of
Octopus Publishing Group Ltd
Carmelite House
50 Victoria Embankment
London EC4Y 0DZ
www.octopusbooks.co.uk

Distributed in the US by
Hachette Book Group
1290 Avenue of the Americas
4th and 5th Floors
New York, NY 10104

Distributed in Canada by
Canadian Manda Group
664 Annette St.
Toronto, Ontario, Canada M6S 2C8

ISBN 978-1-78325-330-2

A CIP catalogue record for this book is available from the British Library.

Printed and bound in China

10 9 8 7 6 5 4 3 2 1

CONTENTS

INTRODUCTION TO THIS GUIDED JOURNAL

Welcome to this guided journal. It is designed to help you discover ways in which you can more effectively transition from the fast pace of the day into a restful evening energy, and it will help you create a space to wind down, stretch out and let go of the day.

The evening is a naturally reflective time of the day, when thoughts can end up going round and round in your head, landing on worst-case scenarios and interpretations. This journal offers prompts to help you integrate any emotions experienced or discoveries made during the day and reflect on how you are feeling through the practice of journaling. The mere act of putting your thoughts onto paper can slow them down enough to allow you to consider them rather than feeling consumed or overwhelmed by them.

The human brain has a tendency to lean toward negative thinking, and so a few minutes of evening journaling is a very helpful tool for developing more positive mental habits. Focusing on gratitude has been shown to increase a person's sense of wellbeing and optimism, and describing the sensations associated with an activity you enjoy, such as how you feel in nature or while chatting to a good friend, offers similar benefits to the activity itself – your body will begin to feel the calm, grounded sensations that you feel in nature, or the sense of connection that you have while talking with a friend.

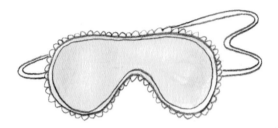

Journaling is an excellent practice for clearing the clutter of your day and your mind. Simply writing down all the to-do lists that are floating around in your head, making you worried, can feel like a great relief.

Many of the prompts and practices in this journal are based on the theme of letting go, as so many of us have a natural tendency to hold on to thoughts and mental or emotional baggage that are no longer serving us. In today's busy world, it can also be helpful to dedicate a few minutes at the end of the day to doing less, to allow your energy to settle and to consider what really matters to you.

The first part of this guided journal is devoted to the practice of embracing the evening and becoming sensitized to the change in pace and energy.

The second part of the journal, Reflect on Your Day, offers prompts to encourage gentle reflection and integration of the day just gone.

In the third part, Where Are You Now?, there are writing exercises for self-enquiry, to help you explore how you are and discover what you need to care for yourself and grow.

And in the final part of the journal, practices are offered to help you prepare for restful and restorative sleep.

AT THE END OF THE DAY

This special time between the day and the night can easily be overlooked, whether we flop down exhausted at the end of the day and watch the latest box set or keep our minds on red alert until we get into bed and then wonder why we can't just go to sleep.

This journal is an invitation, or a permission slip, to cherish your time in the evening. It isn't always easy to do this when it feels like there are a million and one things to get done, but the evening can be the most precious of times in terms of connecting with others, ourselves and the world we live in.

Take a few moments right now to imagine how you would like to spend your evenings if you were able to focus on what helps you to feel relaxed and content.

'The evening star is the most beautiful of all stars.'

SAPPHO

How would you like to spend your evenings?

_____

_____

_____

_____

_____

_____

_____

_____

_____

_____

_____

_____

_____

_____

_____

_____

_____

_____

THE VALUE OF WINDING DOWN & SWITCHING OFF

In our fast-paced world, it's no wonder really that we might need a reminder about the value of slowing down, relaxing and easing our way toward sleep.

Recently there has been much research into the roles of the sympathetic and parasympathetic nervous systems and how we cope with stress. The sympathetic nervous system is designed to respond to stress triggers so that we can act quickly and decisively, helped by the release of adrenalin. This is known as the 'fight-or-flight response'. Conversely, the parasympathetic nervous system, sometimes called the 'rest-and-digest response', regulates the body through processes that restore calm and initiate repairs.

If you can find time in the evening to slow down and do relaxing things, this will help your body transition from the fight-or-flight state into the rest-and-digest phase. Otherwise you run the risk of trying to go to sleep when your body is still feeling stressed, and so might find it hard to fall asleep or notice yourself waking up in the night.

If you remain in the fight-or-flight state, your body will try to compensate for as long as possible, topping you up with extra adrenalin to keep you going when your batteries are almost empty. The problem with this is that you will eventually burn out, which is when the parasympathetic nervous system temporarily collapses and you feel continually tired, even when you are sleeping more than usual.

You can help your body and mind out by bringing the simplest of relaxation practices into your evening routine, such as an aromatic bath or a few minutes of sitting quietly and focusing on your breath.

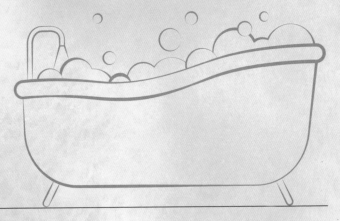

WRITE IT DOWN, THEN LET IT GO

The best times of the day to journal are in the morning and in the evening. Writing your thoughts in a journal at the end of the day encourages the mind to let go of worries, allowing you to focus on how you are feeling, decide what you'd like to prioritize tomorrow or even ask your dreams for guidance.

The Buddhist concept of impermanence is often illustrated by the setting sun or the seasons. The sun is part of the cycle of life: it rises at the beginning of the day and sets at the end, only to rise once again the following morning. It is therefore futile and exhausting to try and cling to the day once it has passed. But of course it is often easier said than done to just 'let go', and writing is therefore one of the best ways to release any thoughts or emotions left over from the day and acknowledge them. This practice in turn develops self-awareness and increases understanding of others. When you explore a situation through journaling, you might discover different ways of looking at a situation, or alternative solutions to a recurring issue.

FIND FIVE
MINUTES FOR YOU

Time has become such a precious commodity in modern life, and
many traditionally restorative practices have been lost, forgotten
or temporarily put away. However, despite the common perception
that there are never enough hours in the day, many people will have
experienced the phenomenon of time expanding or contracting.

You can try this out for yourself right now. On the page opposite, use
the next five minutes to write down the reasons why you picked up this
journal, what you hope to do with it and how you feel about it. Set a
timer but don't look at the time, simply write. At the end of the
exercise, consider how long this tiny period of time felt.

When your mind is focused on just one question, one task or one
experience, you might be amazed at how much time you have.
Journaling for a few minutes has a way of expanding your awareness
generally so that you become more focused and clear-minded,
and even more productive with the time you have.

Evening practices such as lighting a candle or making a cup of sleepy
tea take hardly any time and can also help you to slow down and bring
touches of self-care into your life, allowing you to rest and recharge
for the following day.

YOUR NATURAL RHYTHMS

Depending on your individual body clock, you may be more of a morning or evening person. Your body clock, or circadian rhythm, is your body's master clock, and this inner clock makes sure that your body performs various functions and processes throughout the cycle of a day. If your body clock is slightly less than 24 hours, you are more likely to be a morning person, while if it is slightly longer then it's probable that you will be a night owl.

Surrounded by modern technology, you may find it difficult to tune into your natural energy rhythms, but if you focus on embracing the changes of energy in the natural world, soon you will begin to recognize your own energy patterns. An easy way to do this is to stop using an alarm clock, while on holiday for example, and get up when you wake up. You may discover that you are a natural early riser, and therefore someone who needs plenty of downtime in the evening, or notice that you have high levels of energy in the evening that need a creative or physical output so that you don't go to bed when you are still full of beans.

Make a few notes here about whether you are a night owl or an early bird. How might you be able to adjust your routine to suit your natural body clock?

_____

_____

_____

_____

_____

_____

_____

_____

_____

_____

_____

_____

_____

_____

_____

EMBRACE EVENING ENERGY

We all know that sleep is essential for our health and sense of wellbeing, but often we forget to shift down through the energy gears in the evening, which means that our minds are still in overdrive when we get into bed and we might fall into a less-than-restful sleep.

Evening energy is nourishing and restorative. The evening is an essential time for becoming less active and more receptive. It is the best time to build up our natural resilience, open ourselves to creativity, nurture relationships, check in with how we are feeling and practise self-care. As the light fades, the intensity of the day softens, and as you slow down, you will see more clearly.

BRUSH OFF YOUR CARES

As you step through your front door in the evening, take a few seconds to imagine that you are brushing off all your cares from the day. If you are already home, then find a few moments to do this. Literally use your hands to brush yourself off. Energetically this practice cleanses your aura and psychologically it allows you to begin the process of letting go of the day that has gone and stepping into evening.

Take a moment now to quickly jot down anything you imagine brushing off and make a note of what kind of evening you are looking forward to. Or simply write a few words about how you are.

SOFTEN THE LIGHTS

Nature gives us the most wonderful soothing light as day takes its time to turn into night. Dusk is like a natural dimmer switch, softening the edges and giving us a visual cue to relax.

Follow nature's lead and soften the lighting in your home as the evening arrives. Allow the day that has just been to soften and loosen so that you can reflect gently and let the day ease away.

How does this feel?

_____

_____

_____

_____

_____

_____

_____

_____

_____

_____

_____

_____

_____

_____

_____

_____

_____

_____

_____

TAKE AN EVENING WALK

Weather permitting, taking a stroll in the evening will connect you to your body and to the ground. Even if you are in a city, you might notice the birds enjoying a last burst of chatter or song before settling down, the colours all around you will lose their intensity and the aroma of the earth will become deeper. Slow your pace and just wander, take it all in.

What did you notice on your walk?
Did you meet any animals on your way?

_____

_____

_____

_____

_____

_____

_____

_____

_____

_____

_____

_____

_____

_____

_____

_____

_____

_____

LIGHT A CANDLE
& LET GO

The simple act of lighting a candle somehow makes any evening a little more special. Lighting candles to create a warm glow on dark nights is second nature to Scandinavians during the winter months.

You can turn lighting a candle into a symbolic moment. As you light the candle, focus on letting go of the day (in general or letting go of something specific) or give thanks for both the day and the evening.

What do you wish to let go of?

SLOW DOWN YOUR BUSY MIND

The natural pace of the evening is slower and gentler than the day. Even the energy around us changes from the powerful energy of the sun to the softer light of the moon. Get into the habit of imagining that time itself slows down during the evening hours – there is no need to rush. Slow down your own pace and watch time expand.

If your thoughts are rushing around at full speed at the end of the day, this can leave you feeling drained and exhausted; it can feel impossible to just 'switch off' and relax in the moment.

Writing in a journal for a few minutes in the evening is a meditative exercise that can help to calm a busy mind. Give yourself five minutes to observe your thoughts as they appear and write them down. Just doing this can create a sense of calm and space.

When you have spent a few minutes writing down your thoughts, take a look at your notes. If there is anything here that you feel you need to come back to, schedule a time to revisit those thoughts and then give your conscious mind a break.

SIT & STARE

Set a timer for five minutes and sit quietly. There is nothing to do or
prepare during these few minutes. Nothing at all. Allow your shoulders
to drop, and if you notice you have been breathing shallowly,
or even holding your breath, simply take a few deep breaths and
fully release them with a big sigh.

Your thoughts may drift in and out while you sit and stare – memories of
the day or random recollections. Or you might find that one particular
thought feels like it has taken root and you can't shake it. If that's the
case, imagine where this thought is in your body. What does it feel like?
Go into it. Give it a colour. Perhaps it is linked to a place of tension.
Breathe into it. Don't judge it. Just feel it.

What did you think about in those quiet moments?

_____

_____

_____

_____

_____

_____

_____

_____

_____

_____

_____

_____

_____

_____

_____

_____

_____

_____

_____

_____

WHAT'S THE ALTERNATIVE?

Most of us are skilled in the art of imagining the worst-case scenario. It is like an in-built safety mechanism; we assume that if we have imagined the worst that can happen then we will be prepared if it does.

The problem with this mode of thought is that we spend far too much of our time thinking about possible but unlikely negative scenarios. Some might say that we even get so caught up in these negative thoughts that we don't notice or fully appreciate the good things that come our way.

Look back on your day. Have you been planning for a worst-case scenario? If so, take a few minutes to imagine as many positive alternative scenarios you can think of and write them down.

CREATE A MANTRA

Do you remember learning by repetition when you were at school? Perhaps you used this technique to learn your times tables, spelling or words in a new language? You even learned to walk by constant repetition – if you fall down, get back up again.

Learning through repetition is a method you can apply to your own self-care practices to create a sense of wellbeing. One way to do this is to use a little time in the evening to create a mantra for yourself and write it down repeatedly in your journal to help anchor it for you.

Here are some examples of mantras:

- Only good comes to me.
- I practise self-love every day.
- I am ready for my wishes to come true.

Write down your mantra.

_____

_____

_____

_____

_____

_____

_____

_____

_____

_____

_____

_____

_____

_____

_____

_____

_____

_____

_____

_____

_____

COME INTO THE MOMENT

This journaling exercise releases any hold that the day still has on your thoughts and emotions, bringing you into the present moment.

Grab a pen and settle down with your journal. Casually take a look around you, and notice everything you can see. Focus on an object or a texture or anything you like that strikes you as beautiful. It might not be conventionally beautiful but it has your attention in this moment.

Now describe in the space opposite everything about this object that you see, describe its beauty in detail.

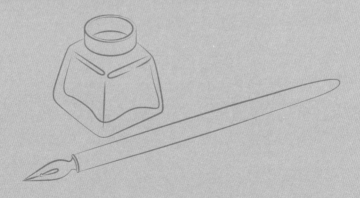

WASHING UP & PUTTING AWAY

Engaging in mindful activities during the evening can bring you into the present moment and signal to your body and mind that now is the time for rest and relaxation in preparation for sleep. This is why sleep routines can be so helpful.

Washing up and putting away after dinner is a wonderful way to help you focus on your senses. These are simple activities that not only bring balance and order into your environment, but also calm the mind, clearing the decks for the following day.

When you wash up, just wash up. Feel the water running over your hands. Notice the bubbles of soap. Wash up with care and a lightness of touch, simply grateful for the food you have enjoyed and attentive to cleaning, drying and putting away the plates, the pots and the pans.

MOON WATCHING & STAR GAZING

Looking up at the moon and the stars is a beautiful way to connect with the 'bigger picture'. According to studies, the sense of awe that we experience when gazing at the night sky even makes us kinder and more compassionate because we are reminded of the presence of something greater than ourselves – something that we are a part of.

This practice naturally encourages us to slow down and embrace a moment of quiet reflection, which can help us to put things back into perspective. We can also simply take a little time to appreciate and be inspired by the beauty of the moon, the stars, and even our own planet. These are the moments in which the magic happens.

Mangata

IS A SWEDISH WORD THAT MEANS

'the reflection of the moon on the water.'

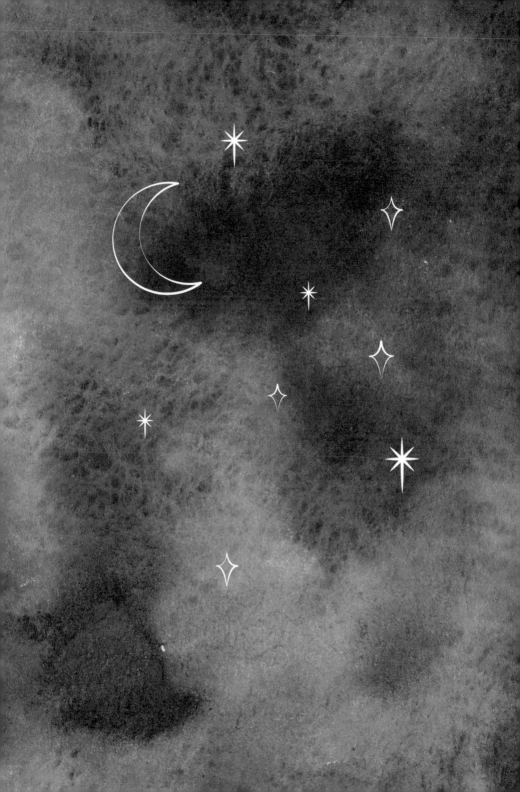

EVENING MINDFULNESS MEDITATION

Here you can write your own script or prompts for an evening mindfulness meditation. You might wish to use the setting sun as your focus, or the tide gently coming in as evening descends, or the gradual appearance of the moon and the stars. Or perhaps you'd like to imagine yourself walking through a magical forest and meeting the animals that live there.

Begin by taking a few slow deep breaths as you imagine descending some steps within your meditation scene, down to a beach or a forest at the end of a garden, for example.

Describe your journey as dusk falls. Use details to engage all your senses: the sounds, the feel of the ground, the sights and aromas in the air.

You may wish to add symbols to your meditation, such as a pebble or shell that you kneel down to pick up as a talisman.

You could drop a question into your meditation, asking for a message at the turning point of your journey. For example, if you are in a forest you might meet an animal and ask if it has a message for you. You can ask for a message from anything in your meditation to which you feel connected, even the waves or a tree.

Now make the return journey and finish by climbing back up the steps, bringing your awareness back into your body and your surroundings.

REFLECT ON YOUR DAY

A few minutes of mindful journaling at the end of the day can help to rebalance your thoughts and perspective. Human beings are quite habitual in their thought patterns, so asking questions is a helpful way to break the patterns and consider the day from all angles. This is why prompts work well for opening up your heart and mind as you put pen to paper.

WHEN DID YOU FEEL ENERGIZED TODAY?

Your energy levels rise and fall through the day according to what's needed from you, and also in response to specific moments, activities and challenges. Perhaps you had a quiet day but felt invigorated by a walk, or you tackled a problem and fired up all your synapses to find the solution, or you had an engaging conversation.

Take a few minutes to remember a time (or times) during the day when you felt energized and describe the sensations. Is it the kind of activity that you might be able to bring into your daily life a little more?

WHAT WENT WELL TODAY?

The human brain tends toward intensifying negative thoughts while quickly dismissing positive ones. The good news is that it's possible to consciously balance things out and develop your inner cheerleader, rather than constantly giving centre stage to your inner critic.

Write down three things that were positive from today.

_____

_____

_____

_____

_____

_____

_____

_____

_____

_____

_____

_____

_____

_____

_____

_____

_____

_____

_____

_____

_____

_____

_____

WRITE DOWN YOUR WORRIES

Studies show that when you write down the anxious thoughts you are having, or have had during the day, the process of writing helps to loosen their grip and intensity. You are putting your worries down instead of holding them tight.

When you look at your worries as words on the page, you might find they don't look quite so scary after all.

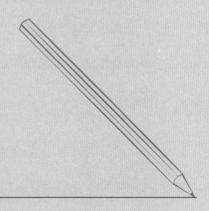

Write down your worries from today.

_____

_____

_____

_____

_____

_____

_____

_____

_____

_____

_____

_____

_____

_____

_____

_____

_____

_____

_____

_____

_____

_____

WHAT DO YOU WISH TO PRIORITIZE FOR TOMORROW?

It can be difficult to sleep when your mental to-do list is swirling around in your thoughts, disturbing your night's sleep or waking you up with a start because you are panicking that you've forgotten something. To avoid this, take a few moments to decide on your priorities for the next day, write them down and get on with the rest of your evening.

Write down up to three priorities for tomorrow.

THANK-YOUS

Each day is made up of so many different moments, and unfortunately the human brain tends toward dwelling on the negatives rather than the positives. When you create a daily habit of saying thank-you to yourself, or writing down a few thank-you notes, you will start to see life from a different perspective, based on gratitude for what is.

Saying thank-you is a powerful habit to cultivate. Gratitude has been shown to be directly linked with improving a general sense of wellbeing and happiness.

'Let us be grateful to the people who make us happy; they are the charming gardeners who make our souls blossom.'

MARCEL PROUST

Write down your thank-you notes.

_____

_____

_____

_____

_____

_____

_____

_____

_____

_____

_____

_____

_____

_____

_____

_____

_____

_____

_____

_____

_____

GET CLARITY

Mindful meditation is a practice that helps you focus on your breath and slow down your thoughts so that you can become the observer. Giving yourself a little bit of space to do this can be very helpful for finding clarity and untangling your web of thoughts and emotions so that a clearer path appears.

Journaling encourages you to investigate how you really feel about a situation, a person or yourself. It enables you to express your thoughts and emotions and then calmly review what you've written.

If there is something or someone in your life that you are uncertain about, or something you know you want to resolve or progress but have become unclear about, give yourself a few minutes to write down all the thoughts and feelings that rise to the surface when you place your attention on this uncertainty. Don't edit yourself, just write it all down.

Read what you have written, imagining that you are a dispassionate but kind observer. What do you notice? What would you suggest to yourself as the next step?

ADVICE FOR A FRIEND

Imagine that a friend is telling you about their day, but actually they are relaying how your own day went. Tune into your inner ear and listen to yourself relaying the events and emotions of the day. If you had any challenging moments or situations, imagine the compassion you would show to a friend. Set aside any self-criticism and offer yourself a little friendly advice or a few words of kindness and encouragement.

REFRAME YOUR FRUSTRATIONS

In the heat of the moment it is easy to let frustrations crowd your thoughts, leaving little room for a calm perspective on the matter. And often there isn't an opportunity to express feelings of frustration when they occur, you just have to push them down and get on with the day.

The evening is a perfect time to take a few moments for quiet reflection on any feelings of frustration you may have felt through the day. The idea of remembering negative thoughts and feelings might not seem pleasant at first, but it allows you to feel the emotion in your body when you are in a safe space, away from the original frustration, and to see it from a more neutral perspective.

RELEASE TENSION

Journaling is a form of expressive writing that can be very helpful for releasing emotional tension. Researchers believe that the combination of thinking about an experience and then writing down the emotions about it can help to give meaning to the experience, which in turn leads to clearer understanding. It is also thought that when we practise expressing how we feel in a private setting, such as in a journal, we are more likely to talk to others if we need support.

Be gentle with yourself if you feel you need to express any tension you have encountered during the day. Write freely and openly in your journal, exploring your feelings, thoughts and emotions. There are no rights or wrongs here.

ENJOY A MOMENT OF PEACE

In this busy world, moments of peace are blessings to be welcomed. Let yourself fall freely into the sensation of peace. Don't be wary of the quiet space that opens up in that moment; peace is restorative to your heart and your soul.

What does peace feel like to you?

DID YOU LEARN ANYTHING NEW TODAY?

This question is a helpful prompt for whenever you are feeling stuck.
Each and every day offers an opportunity to learn something new.
Perhaps you learned an interesting fact or a different way of doing
something, or maybe you learned something about
a person, or yourself.

Buddhist philosophy believes that it is useful to always have a 'beginner's
mind', to be willing to look at the world afresh, to be open and not stuck
in our ways or our thoughts. Take a moment now to reflect on your day.
Did you open up your mind today and welcome in something new?

Today, I learned …

_____

_____

_____

_____

_____

_____

_____

_____

_____

_____

_____

_____

_____

_____

_____

_____

_____

_____

_____

WHAT DID YOU
NOTICE TODAY?

The beauty and mystery of life can be found in the smallest details: the intricate pattern on a leaf, a gentle touch from a friend, a moment of flow during one's work.

As you journal, you will become more aware of and sensitive to these moments. You will experience them not only with your thoughts but also with all of your senses. As you notice more readily how you are feeling, you will observe more easily how others are feeling too. You will see opportunities arising and be more tuned in to your instincts and intuition about different situations.

Today, I noticed…

_____

_____

_____

_____

_____

_____

_____

_____

_____

_____

_____

_____

_____

_____

_____

_____

_____

_____

_____

_____

_____

_____

WHAT QUESTIONS DO YOU HAVE LEFT FROM THE DAY?

Sit quietly for a few minutes and allow any questions from the day to rise to the surface of your mind. For example, this might be an unresolved issue in your work that has been playing on your mind, apparently with no easy solution. Allow yourself to hold any question gently in your thoughts and make a note of it. Ponder it in this contemplative space you have created.

Jot down any words that flash into your mind without stopping to analyse them. If an interesting idea appears, take note, but don't worry if the question remains hanging in the air. Imagine handing the issue over to your unconscious and to the Universe. Hand it over and let go. You might be surprised at what comes back.

LET GO

As you embrace the energy of the evening, imagine yourself loosening your whole body and mind. Breathe gently, deeply and slowly into any tension in your body or worrisome thoughts in your mind.

It's completely natural for the mind to attach itself to worrying thoughts. However, holding onto our worries keeps us in a state of constant alertness, which can be exhausting. Such behaviour can easily become habitual, making even the concept of relaxing or slowing down our minds seem like a distant dream.

Consciously write down any worries or moments of unease, awkwardness or self-criticism from the day. Let these thoughts and emotions flow through your words. Let them go.

WHAT SIGNS DID YOU RECEIVE TODAY?

Did you experience a moment of serendipity or a coincidence that made you smile today? Did you make a decision and allow yourself to sense the answer by listening to your intuition or your gut instinct?

Journaling is a wonderful practice for opening up your awareness so that you are increasingly sensitive to the details in your life and the signs that point the way along your path. As you begin to notice moments of coincidence, you may be surprised by how often they turn up in your life.

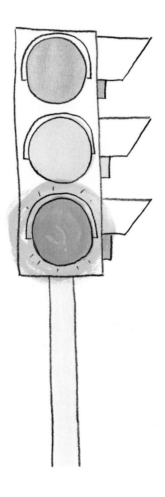

SEND OUT YOUR WISHES

In Reiki, a Japanese form of energy healing, the practitioner calls on the universal energy to flow through them for the highest good of the person they are giving Reiki to. Imagine that your goodwill is like a beam of energy that you can send out into the world. You can send this energy across long distances simply by setting your intention, or you can use your journal to do this by setting down your goodwill in words.

Imagine someone that you would like to send good wishes to right now. Let the words come and flow toward them.

Write down your good wishes.

CHECK IN WITH YOURSELF AT THE END OF THE DAY

The body scan is an excellent mindfulness meditation. It brings you into the present moment and into the energy of the evening and allows you to acknowledge the day and any tension it has left within your body. This act of acknowledgment is a self-awareness practice that encourages emotions to flow rather than create blockages or get stuck in the body.

To do this exercise, you will need a chair and a quiet space where you won't be distracted by people. Noises beyond the space are natural and part of the exercise.

Read through the exercise before you begin as it's best to do this meditation with your eyes closed. You may wish to write a few notes after you've completed the exercise. As you practise it, whether daily or weekly, your experience may change over time.

Sit comfortably with your back straight against the chair and with your feet flat on the ground.

Breathe normally, bringing your attention to your breath.

Gradually bring your attention to the crown of your head and just sense if there is 'presence' here. Try not to 'look' with your mind, but feel this part of your body and notice if there is any energy or sensation there.

Now scan each part of your body in turn, just bringing an awareness rather than looking. How does your right hand feel versus your left? Can you detect a slightly different level of presence? Are there areas of your body where you can't detect any presence? Just notice these areas, there is no need to try and change anything or do anything.

When you have scanned your whole body, gently bring your focus back to your breath. Bring your awareness into the room where you are sitting, and when you are ready, open your eyes.

WHERE ARE YOU NOW?

When you get into the habit of giving yourself a little time for reflection and imagination at the end of the day it not only allows you to process the day that has just been but also helps you to engage in a journey of self-enquiry and explore how you are feeling in your life. Which things are working and should be celebrated more often? What would you like to change or improve? How would you like to live your life?

WHAT DO YOU NEED?

The American psychologist Abraham Maslow is famous for creating a 'hierarchy of needs'. He identified that human beings not only need food and shelter, though these are essential to survival, but also things like connection with other people, love, meaning and purpose.

If you tend to prioritize the needs of others, it can be challenging to focus on asking yourself what you need. However, this is a very important exercise because in order to care for others you first need to be able to care for yourself.

What do you need?

_____

_____

_____

_____

_____

_____

_____

_____

_____

_____

_____

HOW DO YOU TAKE GOOD CARE OF YOURSELF?

The prompt on the previous page encouraged you to consider your needs. It is tempting to think that other people can give you what you need, but doing so means that you can feel hard done by if they aren't up to the task. Rather than relying on other people to meet your needs, you need to be willing to take care of yourself.

On first reflection, that can feel like a huge task, and feelings of lack of self-worth may bubble up to the surface. Start wherever feels comfortable. Consider the ways in which you already take care of your needs. Write down how you can do these things more often.

Which of your needs are you not taking care of? Write down three small steps you can take toward redressing the balance.

WHAT DO YOU WANT MORE OF IN YOUR LIFE?

We are often taught in our childhood that it is wrong to want more –
more cake, more playtime, more television. Developing self-restraint is
a useful habit for certain situations in life, but you might find that this
attitude spills over into rationing the really good things in life, such as
love, fun, spontaneity and even success and money.

'Who would ration success or money?', you may ask. But think about it:
modesty is often praised more readily than success, and money is often
considered to be a slightly distasteful or uncouth subject.

Strip away all such judgments about how you *should* act and feel,
and imagine the life that you dream of.

What do you want in life?

LOVE, LOVE, LOVE

Imagine love in its purest form surrounding you. Ask yourself the following questions:

- What does it feel like?
- Where do you imagine is its source?
- What are its colours?
- What does 'love' mean?

Know that love is yours to give and to receive.

'You don't blast a heart open,' she said.
'You coax and nurture it open, like the sun does to a rose.'

MELODY BEATTIE, *THE LESSONS OF LOVE*

What does love mean to you?

SELF-LOVE

Where are you looking for love? From a lover? From family or friends? You need to begin by loving yourself. Do you shy away from that thought? Do you see only your flaws? Do you wish to be taken care of for once, handing over the responsibility of loving you to others?

How would you like to be loved? Take a few moments to imagine you are able to give yourself all the love that you need. Consider how attractive that self-love might be to others, allowing them to give their love to you freely, with no pressure or demands.

What does self-love mean to you?

ACCEPTANCE

A great deal of mental and emotional energy is spent worrying about things that are out of our control. It can be difficult to accept that this is the case or to surrender control. The words 'acceptance' and 'surrender' don't feel like things to which we should aspire; they suggest that we have given up or been defeated.

Use your journaling time this evening to reflect on the concepts of acceptance and surrender from a different perspective. Consider how freeing it might feel to let go of whatever it is that you feel sure you cannot accept. Explore in your imagination and your body how it might feel to surrender to the flow of the river rather than continuing to hold on to the branch.

Is there anything happening in your life right now that might help you to explore the idea of acceptance?

Today, I choose to accept …

_____

_____

_____

_____

_____

_____

_____

_____

_____

_____

_____

_____

_____

_____

_____

_____

_____

_____

_____

_____

_____

_____

MAKE A DAILY COMMITMENT TO AWARENESS

Take a few minutes to reflect on how aware you were throughout the day and how often you were on autopilot. Did you notice your surroundings? Did you notice how other people were feeling? When people were talking to you, were you more focused on your response than on what they were saying? Were you present?

When you start to observe your levels of awareness, it can be shocking to realize how much time you spend caught up in your own inner-mind chatter, habitual thinking and assumptions. But by observing more, and by reflecting and journaling at the end of the day, you will automatically deepen your levels of awareness and be able to use this as a compass to find your way. You will come to understand the needs of others, and your own, you will sense what you need to do in difficult situations and you will feel more present and receptive in the moment.

Today, I was aware of these moments …

_____

_____

_____

_____

_____

_____

_____

_____

_____

_____

_____

_____

_____

_____

_____

_____

_____

_____

_____

_____

RECEIVE

In Chinese medicine, 'yang' energy is thrusting and active, while 'yin' energy is creative and receptive. The energy of the evening, as the sun goes down and the light fades, is attuned with yin energy, which make it a time to be receptive and receive any wisdom that the experiences of the day have to offer.

The physical act of opening one's hands as if ready to receive can be energetically very soothing after a busy day of doing and giving.

What are you ready to receive?

_____

_____

_____

_____

_____

_____

_____

_____

_____

_____

_____

_____

_____

_____

_____

_____

_____

_____

_____

_____

_____

DROP INTO YOUR HEART & LISTEN

During a few quiet minutes in the evening, reflect on how your actions and decisions during the day have either worked with or against your values, hopes and desires. Don't rush to criticize yourself, but gently check if you feel in alignment (as if your actions and values are going in the same general direction) or if you feel at odds with some of your choices or decisions.

Write whatever comes from your heart.

_____

_____

_____

_____

_____

_____

_____

_____

_____

_____

_____

_____

_____

_____

_____

_____

_____

_____

_____

_____

_____

WHAT BRINGS YOU JOY & TENDERNESS?

Joy can spring from the smallest of moments, such as when you let go of being too serious and become playful, when you laugh until your sides hurt or when you see something that melts your heart. Equally, life is rich in tenderness, which you can experience from the lightest of touches, a smile or a look.

When you think about things that bring you joy or moments of tenderness, you re-experience the sensations and benefit from the feelings of gratitude that come at the same time.

'… a leaf fluttered in through the window this morning, as if supported by the rays of the sun, a bird settled on the fire escape, joy in the taste of coffee, joy accompanied me as I walked…'

ANAÏS NIN, *THE DIARY OF ANAÏS NIN 1944–1947*

What brings you joy?

_____

_____

_____

_____

_____

_____

_____

What brings you tenderness?

_____

_____

_____

_____

_____

_____

_____

_____

_____

LET IN

As much as it is good to let go of what is no longer working for you,
it is equally important to be open to letting new experiences, situations,
ideas and people into your life. It is easy to find yourself existing more or
less within self-imposed limitations. We are all creatures of habit, which
is why asking yourself gentle questions as you journal can be a very
helpful reminder that you might like to expand your boundaries or sail a
little further beyond the confines of your safe harbour.

As you begin to let go and find you have a little more space, whether
in your mind or your heart, consider whether you would like to bring
something new in: more health, more connection, more quiet
or more fun. It's totally up to you.

What, or who, would you wish to let in?

_____

_____

_____

_____

_____

_____

_____

_____

_____

_____

_____

_____

_____

_____

_____

_____

_____

_____

_____

_____

_____

_____

WHAT KEEPS SHOWING UP IN YOUR LIFE?

As you develop your evening journaling practice you may begin to notice the patterns that keep showing up in daily life, including patterns of behaviour that are no longer serving you. There is a school of thought that suggests your outer world is a reflection of your inner world, and so if you keep experiencing something that you don't like, the only way to change the record is to build the courage and commitment to make the change for yourself.

What are you doing over and over again that you wish to let go of?
How could you take one small step in a different direction?
Write your answers on the page opposite.

MAKE A
SELF-CARE
CALENDAR

Instead of your usual to-do list of tasks and jobs, take a few minutes
to make a calendar for moments of self-care that you can plan into
your week or month.

What are your favourite nourishing things to do? Do you love massages
and find them incredibly relaxing but never seem to find the time to
fit them in? Or do you have a favourite place in nature where you feel
renewed by the air and the views? Whatever makes you feel good,
schedule some time for it in your self-care calendar – you can even
draw a little picture of it to remind you.

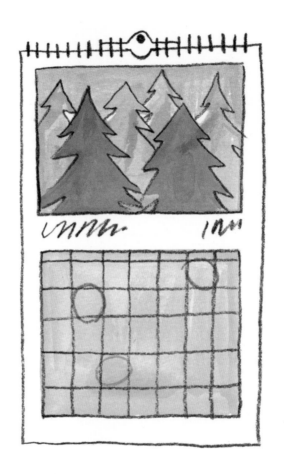

WHAT ARE YOUR DREAMS?

Give yourself permission to go beyond your usual limits.
What is it that you wish for? What would you like to say 'Yes!' to?
What are your dreams? Write the answers to these questions in
your journal. Use your words to expand your ideas in any direction
that takes your fancy.

When you write your dreams (or draw them, if you prefer), you give
them form and substance, bringing them closer to reality and making
it more likely that your actions will lead you toward your dreams,
step by step.

'Wish well. Be well.' **TURKISH PROVERB**

INVITE
YOURSELF TO DO
SOMETHING

Imagine that you are writing yourself an invitation. You can choose
the when and the what, it's completely up to you. You might wish to
invite yourself to something tangible and specific, like a house viewing
if you are currently looking to move. Or it could be an invitation to try
something new or develop an aspect of yourself – to dance or sing,
for example. It could even be an invitation to take a little more time
for yourself, or with a loved one, without the usual daily distractions.

Give yourself a few minutes to imagine what you would like to invite
yourself to do, then write yourself an invitation.

Dear …

I am inviting you to …

_____

_____

_____

_____

_____

_____

_____

_____

_____

_____

_____

_____

_____

_____

_____

_____

_____

_____

_____

_____

_____

EMBRACE THE PROBLEM

If you have come to the end of the day holding a problem in your thoughts, a few minutes sitting with it and embracing it without judgment will bring your subconscious into play. Don't try to think the problem through with a tired mind. Just allow it to be.

If you had to say, where does the problem sit in your body?

Breathe into it, feel it and sit with it quietly.

After a few minutes, if any words come easily that you wish to write down, do so now. Again, no judgment, just let the words flow.

If no words come easily, leave it overnight and see if anything arises in the clear light of a new day.

WRITE A FOUND POEM

A 'found' poem is a simple way of creating a poem using words cut out of a magazine or newspaper. You might see a nice phrase or a quotation and just start putting the words together to see what they form. This is a creative way to play with words and enjoy watching something take shape without knowing where it will go.

Write down your found poem.

STRENGTHEN WHAT IS ALREADY GOOD

Instead of listening to your inner critic, remind yourself about all the positive resources you have. These might include your skills, characteristics, the way you are with other people, the people closest to you and how they support and love you, your passions and interests, your health and your home.

Make a list of all your positive resources, taking time to appreciate each item as you write it down in your journal; or draw a picture of yourself and your resources; or focus your mind on just one of your resources and really feel into it – spreading this good energy through your body.

DEVELOP
SELF-COMPASSION

The evening is a time when self-criticism can rear its ugly head: the moment you find a few minutes to relax and put your feet up, your mind starts to play back a conversation or situation that you believe you could have handled differently, or you begin to fret that perhaps someone might have misinterpreted you, or you worry that you really should have sent an email or made a phone call. The list of reasons to find fault with yourself can feel endless and exhausting, which is why it is essential to develop self-compassion.

Journaling can be a very helpful way to work through these common self-critical thoughts. If you find that you are churning over something from the day in a self-critical way, write down what happened using non-judgmental language. Next, describe your emotions. Finally, write down some words of kindness and encouragement to yourself. After all, you're only human.

LIFE HAPPENS FOR ME

Whatever is showing up in your life and in your day is a reflection of the place where you have a chance to grow.

Consider the concept that life happens 'for' you, not 'to you'.
What lessons did life offer to you today?

WHAT YOU SEEK IS SEEKING YOU

It was the Sufi poet Rumi who said, 'What you seek is seeking you.' His words inspire much exploration and reflection about who we are as individuals and our place in the Universe.

Take a few minutes to just sit with Rumi's words and express whatever comes to you in response.

What is it that you truly seek?

CHECK IN ON YOUR GOALS

The evening is a good time to check in on your big-picture goals and make sure you feel in alignment with them. When you have a little quiet, undemanding time, ask yourself whether there are any small changes you could make to keep your goals on track. If you are feeling out of balance, allow yourself to ask why you feel this way and how it would be possible to come back into alignment. Don't be too quick to judge yourself; this isn't a test, it is just an opportunity to take a little time out from daily life to check in with yourself.

Your goals might include improving your health, spending more time with your family or making your work more effective. If you don't know what your goals are, then explore what these could be. What would you like more of in your life? What is your driving force and how can your life best reflect that?

Write your goals in your journal. Make notes about how to keep yourself on track and stay in alignment with your goals.

ASK THE
ELEMENTALS

Many traditions see twilight as a magical time that exists between day and night. It is often the time when you will see the most animals in the countryside. Twilight brings an energy of transition to the air.

The purpose of journaling in the evening can take many forms, depending on what you need. You can use it to process and let go of the day's events and emotions, to check in on how you are feeling or to express any frustrations that you experienced during the day.

Another option, if it takes your fancy, is to ask the Elementals (the angels, fairies, light beings, trees) to give you signs along your path.

Imagine yourself asking an Elemental for guidance
– and write their response.

Dear …this is what I want to tell you …

_____

_____

_____

_____

_____

_____

_____

_____

_____

_____

_____

_____

_____

_____

_____

_____

_____

_____

_____

_____

ASK YOUR DREAMS TO GUIDE YOU

As evening becomes night and you drift off to sleep, ask your dreams to help answer any questions you may have or resolve dilemmas you are facing. It might seem that your dreams respond with seemingly cryptic clues, but as you develop a journaling practice you may find that your dreams become an interesting part of the problem-solving process. Dreams can also provide inspiration for creativity and new ideas too.

Make a note of your dreams as soon as you wake up, before they drift out of your consciousness. (You might want to use a separate journal or a video recorder to do this.) The meaning of your dreams might not be immediately apparent because dreams are often filled with strange visual associations or symbols, but over time the practice of recording your dreams can be fascinating and illuminating.

What do you wish to ask your dreams?

PREPARE FOR RESTFUL SLEEP

If you find that you are having trouble sleeping, examine both your sleep environment and your routine leading up to going to bed, as there might be ways to create a more soothing atmosphere or help you to wind down before you hit the hay.

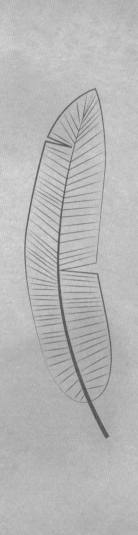

SLEEP DIARY

If you have trouble either going to sleep or sleeping through the night, keeping a sleep diary for a month may help you identify what is keeping you up at night. It will help you spot key patterns, for example whether there are certain foods that seem to disrupt your sleep or particular days of the week (and if you are woman, times of the month) when you have trouble sleeping. You might discover a clear connection between your ability to fall asleep and something as simple as checking your emails after dinner. Or you may realize that you wake up in the middle of the night to the sound of a ticking clock.

Building an awareness of your sleep patterns can be helpful in itself, and you might find yourself doing more of the things that you know are helpful for relaxing at the end of the day.

If you wake up at the same time each night and find that small worries become exaggerated in your mind, making it difficult to feel relaxed enough to fall back to sleep, it can be helpful to turn on a low light, write down your thoughts and then imagine that you are turning them over to the Universe for now. Make yourself a cup of sleepy tea or sip a glass of water and just rest.

CREATING A SAFE SPACE FOR SLEEP

Our nervous system regulates itself best when we feel completely safe. This includes being able to reduce the need for our alert systems to be at the ready. If you keep your smartphone next to the bed and it is lighting up every hour with social-media alerts or incoming emails, even while on silent, then you are less likely to sleep deeply and restoratively.

Don't feel that it is a luxury to spend time making your bedroom as comfortable as possible; it is essential to your health and sense of wellbeing. Keep the lighting levels in your bedroom as low as you feel comfortable with. Ideally, make sure your bedroom is be free from clutter, with clothes tidied away. Bed clothes and bed linen made from natural fibres are optimal because they allow your skin to breathe easily and regulate your temperature.

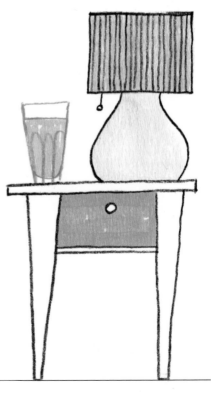

SLEEP MIST

You can make a relaxing aromatherapy sleep mist by adding ten drops of essential oil to a small brown-glass spray bottle, then topping up the bottle with water and sealing the lid. When you are ready to use the sleep mist, shake the bottle and then spray on or around your pillow.

The following essential oils are known for their restful aromas:

- Lavender has sedative properties.
- Cedarwood is thought to relieve tension and stress.
- Frankincense balances negative emotions.
- Marjoram is helpful for clear breathing.

A CUP OF TEA

Drinking a cup of herbal tea after dinner can aid your digestion as well as relaxing you before you head off to bed. There are lots of brands of sleepy teas now available or you can make your own mix.

Ingredients that are often used for sleepy teas include rose, chamomile, lavender, lemon balm and passionflower.

REST & DIGEST

As you may remember, 'rest and digest' is the term used to describe the phase when our parasympathetic nervous system goes into action to regulate and repair the body after the usual stresses and strains of the day (see page 10). This suggests what an important role digestion plays in our health and sense of wellbeing, and of course most of this happens while we are asleep.

You can help your body make the best of this rest-and-digest phase by eating more lightly in the evening, and when possible having an early dinner so that you don't go to bed on a full stomach.

Some foods have sleep-inducing properties, such as lettuce and turkey, but the key is to eat foods that you find easy to digest. Herbs and spices can be very helpful here as they often have properties that aid digestion, including basil, marjoram and cinnamon.

Make a list of favourite foods that you know won't keep you up at night, and also those that are best avoided late in the day.

BREATHE INTO DEEP RELAXATION

This breathing exercise, also known as alternate nostril breathing, will help you relax before you go to bed.

Sit on a chair or on the floor with a blanket or pillow. Feel the crown of your head lift slightly to create a long spine and rest your left hand on your left thigh or knee. Bring your right palm to your nose.

Using your right thumb, softly close your right nostril and inhale as slowly as you can through the left nostril. Using the ring finger of your right hand, softly close your left nostril. Pause. Remove your thumb from your nose and exhale slowly through the right nostril. With the right nostril open, inhale slowly, then close it again with your thumb. Pause. Remove your ring finger from your nose and exhale slowly through the left nostril.

Repeat this sequence ten times, and then lower your right hand to your right thigh or knee. Return to a natural breathing rhythm. If you prefer to use your left hand, go ahead.

STRETCH INTO SLEEP

'Choose forward bends and inversions, as these calm the mind and relax the body,' says yoga teacher Rebecca Oura. 'Back-bends, conversely, can be too stimulating. A good, nurturing sequence could begin with Child's Pose, then move through Cat/Cow, Downward Dog and a gentle spinal twist (lying on your back, knees raised, feet on the floor, arms out at shoulder height; drop the knees to one side, head to the other, and vice versa). Finish by lying on your back, a folded blanket under your hips, and raise your legs at a right angle to your body. You can either rest them against a wall, or use a belt or scarf around your feet. This position stimulates the pineal gland, increasing that all-important evening melatonin production.'

CRYSTALS

Generally, clearing your bedside table of clutter as much as possible helps to create a restful atmosphere for sleep. You might wish to have a small crystal in your bedroom as crystals are beautiful to look at and are thought to have healing energy.

According to energy healer Katie-Jane Wright, the gentlest and most nourishing crystal to have in your bedroom is a rose quartz, as it is very much a crystal for the heart. Other experts suggest that you don't have any pointed crystals in the bedroom but recommend softer shapes. The key is to follow your intuition and observe how well you sleep with a crystal nearby.

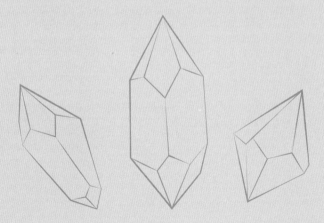

STRESS RELIEF

If you have received bad news, had a shock or feel a bit empty, the Star of Bethlehem Bach flower remedy is considered to be very helpful in alleviating these feelings. This flower essence is even thought to help with healing the effects of trauma suffered in earlier life.

'For those who for a time refuse to be consoled this remedy brings comfort.'

DR EDWARD BACH

TECH RELIEF

The light that is emitted from smartphones and tablets is called 'blue light', and many studies have shown that this type of light can disrupt your inner body clock by slowing down or stopping the natural production of melatonin, the hormone that tells your brain that it's time for your body to sleep. Even if you manage to go to sleep after checking your phone, the quality of your sleep is likely to be affected, and so you might wake up feeling tired.

For a good night's sleep, avoid using blue-light gadgets for 2–3 hours before bed. You might also find that reducing the use of these gadgets in the evening means that you wake up naturally in the morning, without the need to keep an alarm by your bed. And if you like the idea of waking up without a piercing alarm, another option is to purchase a special lamp that gradually wakes you up with light that mimics sunrise.

RESTFUL READING

Sometimes it can be nice to read a meditation script as a way of relaxing into a visualization. Here is a meditation from Ned Morgan's *In the Mountains*.

A MOUNTAIN MEDITATION

Sit on the ground or on a rock in a stable, comfortable position with your body balanced over your hips, your hands in your lap and your shoulders and arms relaxed and free from tension. Close your eyes and start by paying attention to your breath. Don't try to change it, just observe it as it comes and goes. After a minute or two, open your eyes and look around you.

Gradually become aware of the mountain you are sitting on, sensing its magnificence and sheer volume, its top high in the sky and its base rooted in the earth. Feel the shape of the mountain beneath you, its sloping sides and massive weight. As you continue to focus on your breath, feel you are part of the mountain, an ageless presence unmoving yet alive.

Become aware of the patches of light and shade changing on the surface of the mountain as clouds move across the sun, or the sun moves across the sky. Think of gusts of wind buffeting the surface and showers of rain drenching the rock. Imagine clouds plunging the mountain into obscurity, then clearing to allow the sun to warm the rock. The surface of the mountain is continually changing as the weather changes hour by hour, day by day. Yet the mountain is unwavering through time.

We can feel in ourselves that same core of stillness and strength, unmoving despite all the changes and challenges life throws our way. The essence of us remains the same through all the ups and downs, the turmoil and the tranquility. Recognize that sunshine always returns after a storm and, like the mountain, we can remain unmoved.

RESTFUL LISTENING

If you do a lot of listening during the day, then you may benefit from a few minutes of natural quiet in the evening. Alternatively, research shows that listening to a recording of the sound of ocean waves actually changes the wave patterns in your brain, lulling you into a more relaxed state. The ongoing gentle repetition of the sound of ocean waves can help you sleep, meditate or simply bring your body back into a calm state after a hectic day. And if you really love the sound of the waves, listening to the sound of the ocean while working can also boost creativity and concentration.

TREAT YOUR HANDS & FEET

Massaging your hands and feet before you go to bed is the perfect relaxation ritual. Rub some of your favourite lotion or aromatherapy massage oil between your palms and slowly and gently massage your feet or hands – slow movements will help to calm your breathing and your mind as well as ease your muscles.

Do what feels intuitive to you. Using your thumb to press into the centre of your opposite hand, or into the sole of your foot a little above the centre, can be very calming. Gentle massage between the thumb and index finger can be helpful for relieving stress and anxiety.

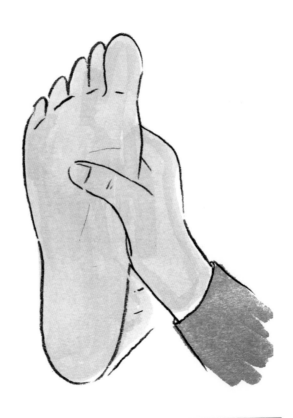

EVENING CHAKRA MEDITATION

This meditation uses the chakras, the seven main energy centres in and around the body according to Vedic tradition. This practice is grounding and relaxing, using colours and different parts of the body to check in with and balance your energy before you go to sleep.

Read through the meditation and then practise it in bed before you go to sleep. You might nod off before you finish the meditation, which is fine!

Get into bed and close your eyes. Take a few moments to focus on your breath, breathing gently and easily, whatever feels right in the moment.

When you feel settled in the rhythm of your breath, bring your attention to your root chakra and visualize energy flowing into and through this red-coloured chakra centre.

Gradually move your attention up through each of the seven chakras: red root, orange sacral, yellow solar plexus, green heart, blue throat, indigo third eye and purple or white crown. Each time gently focus on the area associated with the chakra and visualize energy flowing freely through the centre of the chakra. Take as much time as you wish with each chakra.

Once you reach your crown chakra, enjoy the sensation of balanced energy flowing through and around your whole body.

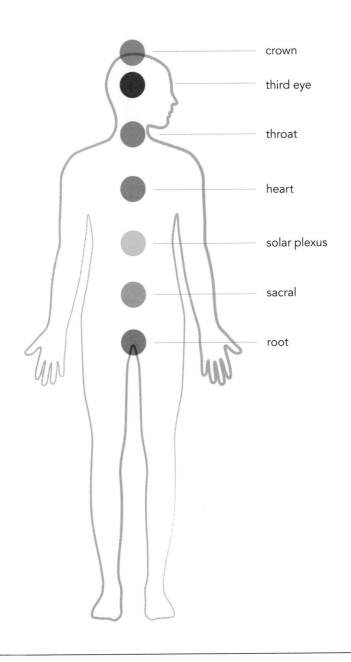

crown

third eye

throat

heart

solar plexus

sacral

root

BRING IN YOUR ENERGY

This is a simple ritual from Chloe Isidora's *Sacred Self-care*.
You can practise it just before you go to sleep to call in your
energy from the day.

As you lie in bed, imagine all the threads of your energy from the
day as threads of light. There will be threads from all the conversations
you have had, the places you have been and the people you have met
or connected to through your phone or computer.

Now, taking gentle breaths from your belly, imagine these threads
of light gradually coming back to you as you call in your energy.
On each exhalation, release the day.

Rest well.

ACKNOWLEDGMENTS

Acknowledgments

p.8, Sapho

p.54, Marcel Proust

p.82, ©Abraham Moslow "A Theory of Human Motivation" 1943

p.88, © Melody Beattie *The Lessons of Love* 1995

p.100, ©Anaïs Nin *The Diary of Anaïs Nin* 1966

p.122, Rumi

p.142, © Rebecca Oura, *Five Minutes to a Healthier You*

p.145, Dr Edward Bach

p.148, © Ned Morgan *In the Mountains* 2019

p.156, ©Chloe Isidora *Sacred Self-care* 2019

Consultant Publisher and words by: Kate Adams
Editorial Assistant: Cara Armstrong
Copyeditor: Clare Churly
Senior Designer: Geoff Fennell
Designer & Illustrator: Ella Mclean
Production Manager: Caroline Alberti